BOMB SQUAD
SPECIALIST

Jil Fine

Children's Press®
A Division of Scholastic Inc.
New York / Toronto / London / Auckland / Sydney
Mexico City / New Delhi / Hong Kong
Danbury, Connecticut

Book Design: Mindy Liu and Michelle Innes
Contributing Editor: Scott Waldman

Photo Credits: Cover and pp. 1, 5, 7, 9, 12, 15, 19, 23, 27, 28, 31, 33, 34, 39 © AP/Wide World Photos; p. 10 © Jeffrey L. Rotman/Corbis; p. 17 © Roger Ressmeyer/Corbis; p. 21 © Allan Tannenbaum/TimePix; p. 25 © Bojan Brecelj/Corbis

Library of Congress Cataloging-in-Publication Data

Fine, Jil.
  Bomb squad specialist / by Jil Fine.
  p. cm. — (Danger is my business)
  Summary: Introduces the type of work, dangers, and requirements for the job of a bomb squad specialist.
  Includes bibliographical references and index.
  ISBN 0-516-24340-3 (lib. bdg.) — ISBN 0-516-27864-9 (pbk.)
  1. Bomb squads—United States—Juvenile literature. 2. Bomb threats—United States—Juvenile literature. 3. Bomb reconnaissance—Juvenile literature. [1. Bomb squads. 2. Bombing investigation—Vocational guidance. 3. Bomb reconnaissance—Vocational guidance. 4. Vocational guidance.] I. Title. II. Series.

HV8080.B5F56 2003
363.2'32--dc21
                                                      2002155011

CONTENTS

You receive a call that there is a bomb threat in the South Glen Mall. You and your partner race to the scene. The police are trying their best to clear hundreds of people from the area. The officer in charge tells you where the suspected bomb is. Your partner helps you into your 60-pound (27.2-kilogram) bomb suit. Bomb suits are heavy and hot, but you've been sweating since you got the call. Even though you've suited up dozens of times before, your job doesn't get any less dangerous. The bomb is thought to be inside a box that was left on a bench in the mall. If the bomb goes off, it could blow you to pieces. It would also kill a lot of innocent people. Your job is to make sure that doesn't happen. Slowly, you approach the box.

Bomb squad specialists are responsible for keeping the public safe from explosive devices. They constantly risk their lives to keep others safe. Read on to find out about the dangerous business of being a bomb squad specialist.

A member of the New York City Police Department's Bomb Squad uses a portable X-ray machine on a boom box that may have a bomb in it.

CHAPTER 1

Lives on the Line

The first recorded bombing plot occurred in 1605. Guy Fawkes was caught sneaking thirty-six barrels of gunpowder into the Parliament building in England. For religious and political reasons, he was attempting to assassinate King James I. Since then, bombers and bombs have become more advanced. As bombs became easier to make, more people started using them to cause terror and violence.

Mind the Mine

More complex bombs became common in the twentieth century. During the early years of World War II, Germany used mines and other explosives against the

In WWII, U.S. Marines used their bayonets to find land mines hidden in the ground.

United States and its allies. Soldiers tried to disarm, or take apart, these explosives. Unfortunately, they were not trained well enough to do the job safely. Military forces around the world began training specialists to deal with these explosives. The first bomb squad school in the United States opened in 1941. In 1951, the navy became responsible for training bomb squad specialists in all branches of the armed forces.

Today, the Bureau of Alcohol, Tobacco and Firearms (ATF) has a bomb squad called the Explosives Technology Branch. The officers in this branch have twenty to twenty-five years of experience as bomb squad specialists. These officers help bomb squads across the nation investigate bombings, defuse bombs, and much more.

Technology Through Time

Bomb disposal, or getting rid of explosives, has always been a dangerous business. Specialists always had to get close to a bomb to dispose of it. It was easy for a bomb to go off in somebody's hand.

ATF agents look for evidence near the site of a bomb blast that destroyed part of a church in Illinois.

This remote-controlled robot is being used by a bomb squad in Jerusalem to investigate a suspicious-looking object.

Technology has helped the job of a bomb squad specialist. Today, bomb squad specialists wear Kevlar bomb suits that are specially designed to protect people in explosions. Kevlar is a lightweight, yet extremely strong material. They also use portable X-ray machines. These machines show what the insides of the bomb they are inspecting look like. Remote-controlled robots also allow the bomb squad specialists to investigate a bomb without being dangerously close to it. Even with these modern advances, a bomb squad specialist's life is always in danger.

Learning From the Past

Bomb squads learn from past bombings. Each bombing teaches important lessons about the changing nature of bomb detection. Bomb squad specialists are able to piece an exploded bomb back together. This helps them find out exactly what kind of explosive was used and how it was built. Bomb squad specialists also use computers to analyze chemicals and other matter left at bomb sites. By learning about the explosives used, they come one step closer to solving the crime.

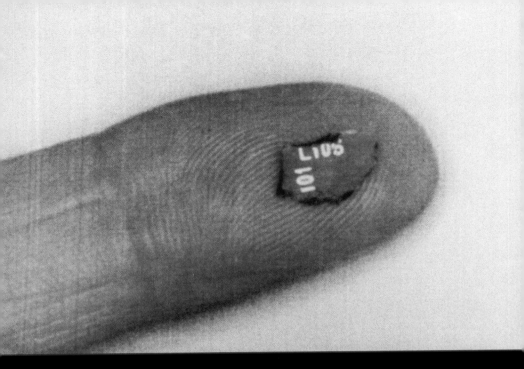

This is one of two bomb fragments that investigators used to find the people responsible for the destruction of Pan Am flight 103.

In 1988, Pan Am flight 103 exploded over Lockerbie, Scotland. Two hundred and seventy people were killed. A bomb was thought to be the cause of the explosion. Investigators were able to use two small pieces of the bomb they found to bring the people responsible to justice. In 1995, a bomb destroyed a building in Oklahoma City, Oklahoma. The ATF bomb squad searched through the Oklahoma City wreckage. In only ten days, they were able to build a model of the 4,800-pound bomb used in the bombing. This helped bomb squad specialists figure out that the bomb was delivered to the site in a large truck. This information helped investigators find who was responsible for the bomb.

The ATF has a database with information on every bombing case since 1974. It includes how the bomb was made, who made it, and special features of the bomb. About eighty thousand bombings are in the database. Bomb squad specialists can save more lives when they know what they're up against.

CHAPTER 2

Doing What It Takes

What type of person becomes a bomb squad specialist? It's definitely someone who enjoys living life with danger only a step away. Often, people who enjoy fixing gadgets and working with technology make excellent bomb squad specialists. They have to be intelligent people who can figure out how complex devices work. Taking apart a bomb is a complex three-dimensional puzzle. If a bomb squad specialist makes one false move while he or she is attempting to solve that puzzle, it can mean death for many innocent people.

Bomb squad specialists must be willing to risk their lives. They must work well under extreme pressure. They must also be patient and work well with others.

These policemen in Reno, Nevada, have the dangerous job of cutting off the top of a bomb so that its contents can be disposed.

The bomb squad is a team in which every person involved is responsible for the lives of the others. A bomb squad specialist must also be in excellent physical condition. He or she cannot be overweight, have high blood pressure, or have poor hearing. Imagine if a doctor had to rescue a bomb squad specialist who has had a heart attack or fainted. Many lives would be in danger. Bomb squad specialists for local police departments must have at least five years of experience in the police force. They also need to be recommended by their supervisors. Military bomb squad specialists must also be recommended before they can be admitted into bomb squad training.

Police Bomb Squad Training

Police department bomb squads train at the Federal Bureau of Investigation (FBI) Hazardous Devices School. The school is located at the U.S. Army's Redstone Arsenal in Huntsville, Alabama. The school was created in 1971. The school has firing ranges, and test pits in which to explode bombs. There is also a

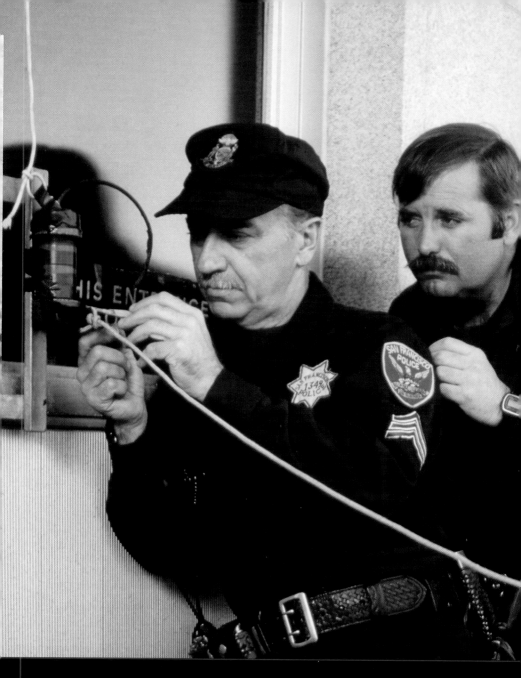

A bomb squad trainee practices defusing a fake bomb while his trainer watches closely.

booby-trapped shack, and a trailer that is used to train officers about the dangerous chemicals used to make illegal drugs. Each class has twenty-four students. Thousands of police officers from across the country have become certified bomb squad specialists since the school opened. Today, there are 435 certified bomb squads in the United States. Some students have to wait up to a year and a half before they are able to go for training. After students complete their training, they must get recertified every three years. They also must have 40 hours of training in explosives each year. Students can stay one step ahead of the bombers by studying many different types of explosives.

Bomb Practice

The training at Redstone lasts for five weeks. In the first two weeks of training, students learn about standard explosives, such as C4 and dynamite. They also learn about homemade bombs and different fuses used to cause explosions. Students learn to use equipment such as X-ray machines and robots to find and get rid of bombs.

This bomb squad specialist uses a training kit to learn how to take apart complex bomb devices used by terrorists.

Students complete several drills that teach them how to work and be comfortable in their bomb suits. One drill is called the "dead bug." The student puts on a 60-pound (27.2-kg) bomb suit and lies on the ground. Then the student must quickly get back on his or her feet. In further training, students must also be able to unscrew the top off a box without moving it.

They do this while inside the suit. If a student upsets the box in any way, a red light inside will go on. This signals that if the box were a bomb, it would have exploded. Each student must also be an expert at using a disruptor. A disruptor is a device used to shoot water, beanbags, or other items at a bomb to disconnect its power supply. Batteries are a common power supply for bombs. Students must also know how to use bomb containment vessels. Bomb containment vessels are portable containers in which some types of bombs are destroyed. Specialists blow up bombs that they cannot disarm in bomb containment vessels.

Beware of Booby Traps

Students must also perform well in several life-like scenarios at Redstone. One training section is a booby-trapped area called Room 402. Room 402 is actually three rooms with trip wires that cause explosions when touched. Room 402 also has trick floors that explode when stepped on. There are also doors that explode when opened. The object of Room 402 is

The New Jersey State Police explode bombs they are unable to take apart in this portable container.

to teach students to identify and avoid different types of booby traps.

The Hazardous Devices School also teaches students how to examine an area after a bomb has exploded. Students are taught to search for even the smallest clues about the bombing. This way they will have a better chance of catching the bomber.

Recently, a model strip mall, train station, farmhouse, and residential area were added to the Hazardous Devices School. These additions will prepare bomb squad specialists for what they will face in the real world.

K-9 on Patrol

Dogs are also trained to help bomb squads find explosives and save lives. Dog handlers are selected based on their police or military experience, physical condition, and their knowledge of dogs. They do not disarm bombs.

Dogs can find explosives more quickly and accurately than any machine. They have forty-four times the sniffing power of humans. Dogs can be trained to detect nineteen thousand kinds of explosives. German Shepherds and Labrador Retrievers are used most often in bomb squads. Both breeds are known for their intelligence. Only dogs that are between one and three years old are trained. Males are generally used to find

Both the FBI and ATF use dogs to help them in their work—from tracking down criminals to finding unexploded bombs.

explosives. This is because they are more aggressive than females. Most dogs are taught to sit down when they smell an explosive. Dogs are taught to learn about fifteen different scents. To teach them, dog handlers expose the dog to each scent about one hundred times. Whenever the dog is correct, it is rewarded with food, play, or praise.

Military Training

The military has a much longer training for their bomb squad specialists. Most military bomb squad specialists are trained for almost a year. Much of the training is done by the navy at Eglin Air Force Base in Florida. Officers must be trained in ground, air, homemade, and nuclear explosives. In addition to the type of training police officers receive, military bomb specialists must be able to locate and disarm unexploded rockets. Part of the training is in the type of weapons and explosives that can carry deadly diseases or poisons.

RISKY BUSINESS

Richard L'Abbé is president of Med-Eng Systems, a company that makes bomb suits. He has exposed himself to explosions nineteen times while testing his suits!

This bomb defuser has found a small stash of explosives in war-torn Bosnia that could still harm innocent people.

One very important part of military training is learning how to find and defuse land mines. Students must check for booby traps, dig up the mine with their hands, and use a rope to slide it out of its hole. The students must work very slowly. If they make a mistake, a quarter pound of TNT, a powerful explosive, that is hidden nearby will explode. Fake explosions cover the student in water and mud. This signals that if the mine had been real, it would have exploded in his or her hands.

Testing Time

When they have finished their training, the students are tested. If they don't pass the 90-minute test the first time they take it, they can take it the next day. If they fail again, they must go before a review board. This board is a group of experienced bomb squad specialists who decide if the student can stay in the program.

Even though this dolphin likes to play, it is being trained to do serious work such as finding underwater mines.

RISKY BUSINESS

The U.S. Navy trains dolphins, sea lions, and whales to help them find underwater mines. The animal finds the mine and attaches a device to it. Part of the device floats to the surface, making it easy for the navy to find the mine.

Biological bombs can kill many people before they are even detected. The foam in this photo is used to cover up the deadly disease anthrax, which can be carried by biological bombs.

In the NEST

In order to combat nuclear terrorism, the U.S. government created the Nuclear Emergency Search Team (NEST). Since 1975, NEST has responded to more than one hundred nuclear threats. The members of NEST are from military bomb squads who are specially trained in nuclear, chemical, and biological bombs. Biological bombs carry deadly diseases. Chemical bombs release hazardous poisons and gases. NEST uses much of the same equipment as other bomb squads. If radiation escapes from the bomb, they build a 50-foot (15.2-meters) wide, 35-foot (10.7-m) tall tent around it. NEST officers fill the tent with foam to trap the radiation if the bomb leaks or explodes. If the officers cannot defuse the bomb mechanically, the NEST officers have to defuse it by hand. This means that NEST officers must go inside the foam. They wear special suits that allow them to breathe while in the foam. Then, they defuse the bomb by hand. This is especially difficult since the bomb squad specialists cannot see anything while in the foam.

Always More to Learn

Bomb squad specialists must always learn new ways to find and disarm bombs of all types. The FBI Bomb Data Center shares new bombing information with others. Bomb squad specialists consult FBI resources as well as others to stay informed about bombs in the world. Terrorists don't rest—and neither can bomb squads around the world.

Robots such as this one are now being used by the U.S. military to find bombs in areas that are too dangerous for soldiers.

CHAPTER 3

A Day in the Life

One Day at a Time

A call comes in to the police bomb squad team in Jessup County. Two specialists on duty, Ralph and Victoria, respond immediately. They race in the bomb truck to a nearby train station where a mysterious package was found. The truck has all the equipment the bomb squad specialists will need to face danger at the site. Police are trying to clear the people out of the station when the specialists arrive.

When he called the police, the bomber said that the bomb was on track three. No one knows when the bomb will go off—there is little time to waste. Quickly, the bomb squad specialists search the area for

This bomb squad specialist suits up to check for bombs at the 2001 New Year's Eve celebrations in Times Square, New York City.

These bomb squad specialists are X raying a suspicious package placed near a political meeting.

booby traps. They divide the area into three horizontal sections, working from the ground up. First, they search from the floor to their waist. Then, they search the area from their waist to their chin. Finally, they search the area from their chin to the ceiling.

When they have determined that there are no booby traps, the K-9 team is brought into the area. The dog handler's name is Erin. Erin and her dog Rudy search the entire area. Rudy sniffs the ground excitedly. Rudy and Erin check along the walls and anywhere a bomb might be hidden. Suddenly, Rudy sits down next to a bench. He has picked up the scent of an explosive. The bomb has been located. It is in a suitcase hidden under the bench.

Ralph helps Victoria get into her bomb suit. It takes almost 5 minutes for Victoria to put on her suit. Victoria carefully puts the portable X-ray machine as close as she can to the suitcase without touching it. When she has taken a X-ray image of the bomb, Victoria hurries back to the bomb truck to study it. Victoria and Ralph use the X-ray image to figure out how the bomb was made so they can disarm it. After viewing the image, they decide to use the robot to open the suitcase.

Victoria operates the robot. A bomb squad specialist's hands are not covered. This allows the specialist to easily operate equipment and perform other tasks. From about 200 feet (60.9 m) away, Victoria directs the robot to the bomb. The robot has cameras on it so that Victoria can see what she is doing. Victoria carefully directs the robot arm to open the suitcase. She can see the bomb clearly. Luckily, the power source of the bomb is also visible. Victoria and Ralph quickly agree that it would be best to use the disrupter to defuse the bomb. Their robot has a disrupter attached to it. Victoria uses the laser sighting on the disrupter to line up exactly where she wants to hit the bomb to defuse it. Victoria fires the disrupter. Water flies out at 800 miles (1,287 kilometers) per hour. It knocks the fuse from the bomb. Victoria and Ralph breathe a little easier. The bomb will not go off. Everyone will go home in one piece.

Bomb squads around the country are called into action every day. The Los Angeles Police Department Bomb Squad alone gets about nine hundred calls each year. That's almost three calls each day! Not all bomb threats are true, but until a bomb squad specialist knows that a package isn't a bomb, it must be treated as if it is real.

RISKY BUSINESS

A common pipe bomb can kill someone 300 feet (91.4 m) away. Pieces of a bomb can travel 3,000 feet (914.4 m) per second.

CHAPTER 4

Bombs of the Future

Bomb squads have been especially hard at work since the terrorist attacks of September 11, 2001. Since January 2002, NEST has randomly searched cities in the United States for nuclear bombs. Almost every week since then, up to six NEST members search docks and other crowded areas. They carry special detectors to alert them if nuclear matter is nearby.

New Threats

New threats come in every day and bomb squads must be ready to face them. Nuclear weapons are a major concern for bomb squad specialists today. Dirty bombs are explosives that have radioactive material on them. Terrorists who are unable to build a nuclear bomb may

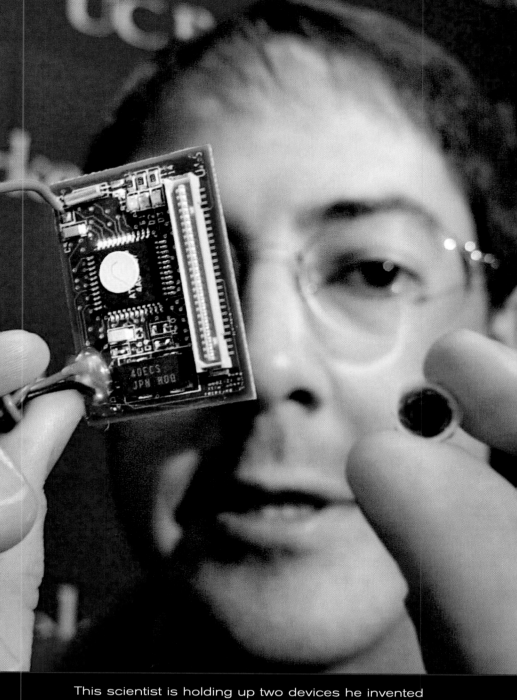

This scientist is holding up two devices he invented to detect the type of deadly chemicals released into the air by chemical bombs.

choose to make a dirty bomb. Dirty bombs may not cause as much damage as a nuclear bomb, but they are still very dangerous.

Bomb squads across the United States are also getting more training on how to deal with the type of weapons that carry deadly diseases and poisons. They must know what these weapons look like and how to defuse them without releasing any poisons into the air. Local bomb squads work with special military bomb squads, who are trained to get rid of these weapons safely. Bomb suit makers have even created special suits that protect the bomb squad specialists from diseases and poisons.

Today, bomb squads are busy saving lives across the world. Military bomb squads are in places like Kuwait and Bahrain in the Persian Gulf. They are hard at work in war-torn areas getting rid of rockets and mines that have not exploded, but are still dangerous. Local bomb squads respond to hundreds of calls each year and are constantly researching new bomb-building techniques.

Science of the Future

Scientists and engineers are busy, too. They are developing new technology to help bomb squad specialists do their jobs. Scientists in California have developed a substance called smart dust that glows when there are chemicals in the air. In the future, this smart dust could help bomb squad specialists find harmful chemicals and save lives. Today, airports across the country are testing new machines that check passengers for explosives by testing the air around them. Robots can now be operated by remote, or be programmed to travel from one place to another without anyone's help. In the future, robots will be able to do many things, such as find bombs inside bags, without needing a person nearby to operate them. The further away bomb squad specialists are from the bombs they dismantle, the safer they will be. Hopefully, many lives will be saved with more accurate and advanced technology.

Bomb squad specialists must confront new dangers everyday. Through study and hard work, they try to stay one step ahead of the bombers and terrorists of the world.

allies (**al**-eyez) groups or countries that give support to one another

analyze (**an**-uh-lize) to examine something carefully in order to understand it

assassinate (uh-**sass**-uh-nate) to murder someone who is well-known or important

bayonets (**bay**-uh-net) a long knife that can be fastened to the end of a rifle

booby trap (**boo**-bee **trap**) a hidden trap or explosive device that is set off when someone or something touches it

database (**day**-tuh-bayss) the information that is organized and stored in a computer

defuse (dee-**fyooz**) to make a bomb safe so that it cannot explode

dispose (diss-**poze**) throwing away or recycling something

explosive (ek-**sploh**-siv) a substance that can blow up

fuse (**fyooz**) a cord or wick leading from a bomb that is lit to make the bomb explode

investigator (in-**vess**-tuh-gate-ur) someone who finds out as much information as possible about a crime

mine (**mine**) a bomb placed underground or underwater

nuclear (**noo**-klee-ur) to do with the energy created by splitting atoms

pipe bomb (**pipe bom**) a bomb made inside a pipe

portable (**por**-tuh-buhl) able to be carried or moved easily

remote-controlled (ri-**moht**-kuhn-**trohld**) using a system for operating machines from a distance, usually by radio signals, or by a light beam

suspicious (suh-**spish**-uhss) to feel that something is wrong or bad

TNT (**tee**-ehn-tee) an explosive; also called dynamite

X ray (**eks ray**) an invisible high-energy beam of light that can pass through solid objects and is used to take pictures of the insides of something

George, Charles, and Linda George. *Police Dogs.* Mankato, MN: Capstone Press, 1998.

Greenberg, Keith Elliot. *Bomb Squad Officer: Expert With Explosives.* Woodbridge, CT: Blackbirch Marketing, 1995.

Singer, Marilyn. *A Dog's Gotta Do What a Dog's Gotta Do: Dogs at Work.* New York: Henry Holt & Company, 2000.

Smith, Gary R. *Demo Man: Harrowing True Stories from the Military's Elite Bomb Squad.* New York: Pocket Books, 1997.

Tomajczyk, Stephen F. *Bomb Squads.* Osceola, WI: Motorbooks International, 1999.

Web Sites
Bureau of Alcohol, Tobacco and Firearms (ATF): Kid's Page
www.atf.treas.gov/kids/index.htm
Read about the history of the ATF, the canines that work for the ATF bomb squad, and more on this Web site.

FBI Youth
www.fbi.gov/kids/6th12th/6th12th.htm
This Web site has information about the FBI, including the dogs that help them find explosives.

PBS: Nova: Bomb Squad
www.pbs.org/wgbh/nova/robots/
Learn about robots that are used in bomb squads and new technology of the future on this Web site.

Organizations

Federal Bureau of Investigation

J. Edgar Hoover Building
935 Pennsylvania Avenue, NW
Washington, D.C. 20535-0001
(202) 324-3000
www.fbi.gov

Naval School of Explosive Ordnance Disposal

304 N. McCarthy Avenue, Suite 117
Eglin Air Force Base, FL 32542

About the Author

Jil Fine is an editor and freelance writer living in New York City.